THE SCIENCE BEHIND

Communication

Casey Rand

Chicago, Illinois

www.capstonepub.com
Visit our website to find out more information about Heinemann-Raintree books.

To order:
☎ Phone 888-454-2279
🖥 Visit www.capstonepub.com
to browse our catalog and order online.

Edited by Megan Cotugno and Laura Knowles
Designed by Richard Parker
Picture research by Mica Brancic
Original Illustrations © Capstone Global Library Ltd 2012
Illustrations by Oxford Designers & Illustrators

Originated by Capstone Global Library Ltd
Printed and bound in China by Leo Paper Products Ltd

15 14 13 12 11
10 9 8 7 6 5 4 3 2 1

Library of Congress Cataloging-in-Publication Data
Rand, Casey.
  Communication / Casey Rand.
      p. cm.—(The science behind)
  Includes bibliographical references and index.
  ISBN 978-1-4109-4485-6 (hc)—ISBN 978-1-4109-4496-2 (pb) 1. Wireless communication systems—Juvenile literature. I. Title.
  TK5103.2.R348 2012
  621.381—dc23   2011014565

Acknowledgments
We would like to thank the following for permission to reproduce photographs: Corbis pp. **10** (Lebrecht Music & Arts/© Lebrecht Authors), **11** (© Bettmann), **17** (ClassicStock/© Camerique), **19** (© Atlantide Phototravel/Stefano Amantini); ESA p. **21**; Shutterstock pp. **5** (© Oliveromg), **7** (© Pablo77), **8** (© Trombax), **9** (© Patricia Hofmeester), **12** (© Jhaz Photography), **14** (© Ericlefrancais), **25** (© Monkey Business Images).

Cover Image of a communications satellite in space reproduced with permission of ESA.

We would like to thank David Crowther and Nancy Harris for their invaluable help in the preparation of this book.

Contents

Look for these boxes:

Stay safe
These boxes tell you how to keep yourself and your friends safe from harm.

In your day
These boxes show you how science is a part of your daily life.

Measure up!
These boxes give you some fun facts and figures to think about.

Some words appear in bold, **like this**. You can find out what they mean by looking at the green bar at the bottom of the page or in the glossary.

Communication

Ring, ring! A **telephone** call can be exciting. Imagine a world without phones. Hundreds of years ago, if you wanted to talk to someone in a faraway place, you might have had to pack your bags and travel. Before planes, trains, and cars, this could take months or even years!

What is communication?

Communication can be a wink, a thumbs-up, a wave, or a smile. A phone call, email, or text message is communication, too. There are many forms of communication. Any way in which thoughts, ideas, messages, or information is shared is communication.

Did humans invent communication?

New inventions have changed the way in which we **communicate**. However, humans did not invent communication. Animals have been communicating with sounds, smells, color, and movement since long before humans were around.

telephone   device that changes sound into signals and sends it to distant places, and then changes signals back into sound

Telephones make talking to friends in faraway places fast and easy.

communication   exchange of messages, thoughts, ideas, and information
communicate   exchange messages, thoughts, ideas, and information

Language

The letters on this page are **symbols**. Symbols have special meaning. When you read these letters out loud, the sounds you make have special meaning, too. These sounds and symbols are **language**.

Life without language

Language makes **communicating** with others easier. Imagine being in a faraway place where everyone speaks a different language from you. Asking for directions to a store would be very difficult! Language allows us to share ideas and information with those around us.

In your day

Learning to read and write takes lots of practice. However, it is easier today than it was thousands of years ago. In English, you have to memorize 26 letters. These form every word. Before the alphabet, a symbol was memorized for each word. So, hundreds or thousands of symbols would need to be memorized.

symbol   something that represents something else, such as letters
language   set of sounds and symbols and the rules for how to use them for communication

Many animals have their own languages. Birds sing, dogs bark, and lions roar.

Long Distance

Sending a letter to a friend today is easy. You can mail a written message across the country, or even across the world, in just a few days. Sending mail across the world has not always been so easy.

Today, all you need to send a message is a stamp and a postcard or envelope.

Marathon messengers

For thousands of years, **messengers** carried news and **communication** on foot. The most famous messenger was named Pheidippides. He ran 25 miles (40 kilometers) to deliver news of the Greek victory at the battle of **Marathon**! Today, there is a long running race called a marathon, in memory of the messenger's amazing effort.

messenger   anyone who delivers a message
marathon   long running race named after an ancient Greek village

Pony Express

Before planes, trains, and cars, many important messages were delivered on horseback. During the 1800s, a mail service called the Pony Express was formed in the United States. Pony Express stations were about 10 miles (16 kilometers) apart across the West. Messages were carried by riders on horseback, who would change to a fresh horse at every station.

This postage stamp was made in memory of the famous Pony Express.

Extra! Extra! Read All About It!

Hundreds of years ago, all books were written by hand! Copying a book by hand takes a very long time. Because of this, books were very expensive. Most people could not afford to buy their own books. Since very few people had their own books, not many people at this time ever learned to read.

Printing machines

A **printing press** is a giant machine that makes **print**. Print is markings or letters made on paper, like the letters in this book. One of the first printing presses was invented in the country of Germany in the mid-1400s.

The printing press made books and newspapers widely available for the first time.

printing press   machine that allows fast printing of books and newspapers
print   markings or letters made on paper

Newspaper

The printing press made it possible to print newspapers. The first newspapers were printed in the 1600s. There was no radio, **television**, or **Internet** at that time. Newspapers quickly became the best place to find news and information.

On days when there was big news, newspaper sellers used to cry out, "Extra! Extra! Read all about it!"

television   device that converts signals into moving pictures and sounds
Internet   system that connects millions of computers around the world

11

Communication: It's Electric!

Communicating with anyone who lived far away used to be very slow. Then, bingo! Humans learned how to use **electricity**.

Electricity

Electricity is a carrier of energy. A flash of lightning during a storm is electricity. This flash may seem to only last a second, but a lightning bolt can travel more than 5 miles (8 kilometers) during this flash. Electricity travels very fast.

Lightning is a flash of electricity that moves quickly across the sky. Electricity can be used to carry messages from one place to another very quickly.

electricity   form of energy on which information and communications can be sent extremely fast, through wires

Beep, beep! It's the telegraph

The **telegraph** was invented by U.S. inventor Samuel Morse in 1837. This machine allowed pulses (beats) of electricity to be sent along a wire. These pulses were a series of short and long beeps. The beeps made up a special alphabet called **Morse code**. Messages could be sent very quickly using Morse code and electricity.

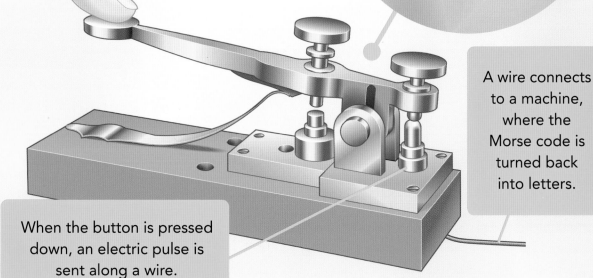

A person taps out Morse code by pushing down on the button for a short or long time.

The button of a telegraph machine was pushed to make short and longer beeps. These beeps raced through a wire, using electricity, to the place the message needed to be sent.

A wire connects to a machine, where the Morse code is turned back into letters.

When the button is pressed down, an electric pulse is sent along a wire.

telegraph device that sends and receives electric pulses, usually in Morse code, to allow communication

Morse code code of short and long beeps used to send messages via telegraph

Ring, ring! It's the telephone

A ringing **telephone** can be very exciting. Who could be calling? A friend, a family member, or someone with good news?

Talk to me

While sending messages in Morse code was fast, people wanted to hear each other's voices. In the 1870s, Scottish inventor Alexander Graham Bell found a way to use a telegraph line to send the sound of his voice. Soon everyone would be using telephones.

Telegraphs and telephone calls traveled on electrical wires. By the late 1800s, these wires connected major cities around the world.

Going global

Telegraphs and telephone calls had to travel along an electrical wire. So how could a message travel all the way from the United States to the United Kingdom, across the Atlantic Ocean? An electric wire had to be laid all the way across the ocean floor! This wire allowed the first telegraphs and phone calls to be sent across the oceans.

Measure up!

Morse code is a **language** made up of short and long beeps. On paper, the short beeps are shown as dots, and the long beeps are shown as dashes. Here is the Morse code alphabet:

A	·—	B	—···	C	—·—·
D	—··	E	·	F	··—·
G	——·	H	····	I	··
J	·———	K	—·—	L	·—··
M	——	N	—·	O	———
P	·——·	Q	——·—	R	·—·
S	···	T	—	U	··—
V	···—	W	·——	X	—··—
Y	—·——	Z	——··		

Can you figure out what this Morse code message says?

·—· · ·— —·· ·· —· ——·

·· ···

··—· ··— —·

Television Time

Watching **television** can be very exciting. There are speeding cars, racing trains, distant places, and fairy tales. Television is amazing. But what is even more amazing is the science behind television. A film camera on the other side of the world can capture sounds and pictures of what is happening at that moment. These sounds and pictures can travel almost instantly to your television!

Picture this

When you have your school photograph taken, this is a **still picture**. Still pictures are images that do not move. Many magazines, newspapers, and books are filled with still pictures.

In your day

What do still pictures have to do with television? When you watch television, it looks like a moving picture. In fact, television is just many still pictures taken one after another. Still pictures are flashed on the screen of your television so quickly that they blend together to look like a moving picture.

still picture   image or picture that does not move

Wireless Revolution

These days we can talk on **telephones** in the park, listen to the radio in the car, and check email from a train. We do not need wires to **communicate**. **Communication** has gone **wireless**.

Radio waves

Radio waves, like **electricity**, are a form of energy. They can carry messages and information. But radio waves do not travel on a wire. They travel through air. They are invisible and silent, but they are all around us.

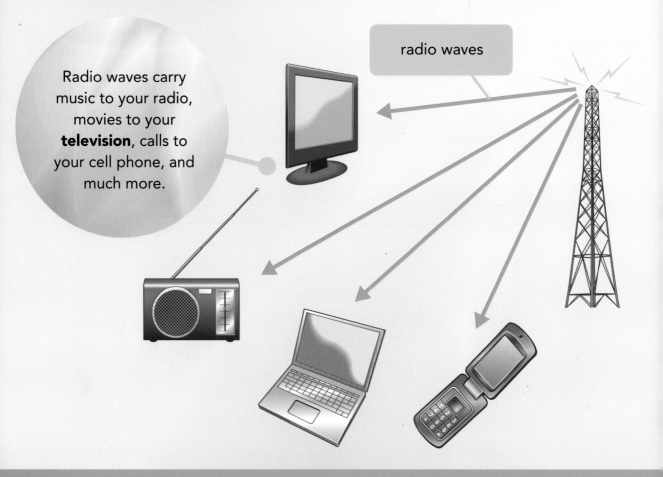

Radio waves carry music to your radio, movies to your **television**, calls to your cell phone, and much more.

radio waves

wireless   signals that can be sent without the use of cords, cables, or wires—usually using radio waves

Calling all readers

For almost 100 years after phones were invented, they had to be connected to a wire. People could not take their phones with them. The **cell phones** of today use radio waves. Now phones can go almost anywhere.

Today's cell phones can be used almost anywhere.

radio wave   type of energy that carries information through the air
cell phone   phone that sends wireless signals by radio waves

Space satellites

If you look up at the night sky, you might see a tiny, fast-moving light. You may think this is a shooting star or falling comet, but it is probably a **communications satellite**. These are devices made for communication that fly high above Earth. The satellites send and receive information all around the world.

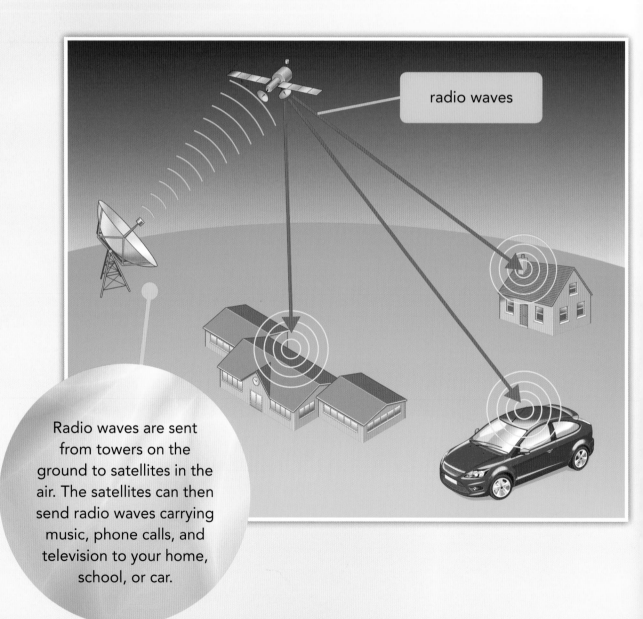

radio waves

Radio waves are sent from towers on the ground to satellites in the air. The satellites can then send radio waves carrying music, phone calls, and television to your home, school, or car.

communications satellite device that flies high above Earth and sends and receives communications to and from Earth

Gravity keeps satellites like this one flying around and around Earth.

Flying around Earth

Have you ever wondered why the Moon moves around Earth? The answer is **gravity**. Gravity is what pulls you back to Earth when you jump. It also keeps the Moon flying around Earth. The pull of gravity keeps communications satellites from flying off into outer space.

gravity   natural force that pulls you back to Earth when you jump

The Internet

Have you used a computer to order pizza, or to find out information about elephants? When you use a computer to do these things, you are using the **Internet**. The Internet connects millions of computers around the world so they can share information. It lets us **communicate** with friends and family, and also to find out information about almost anything!

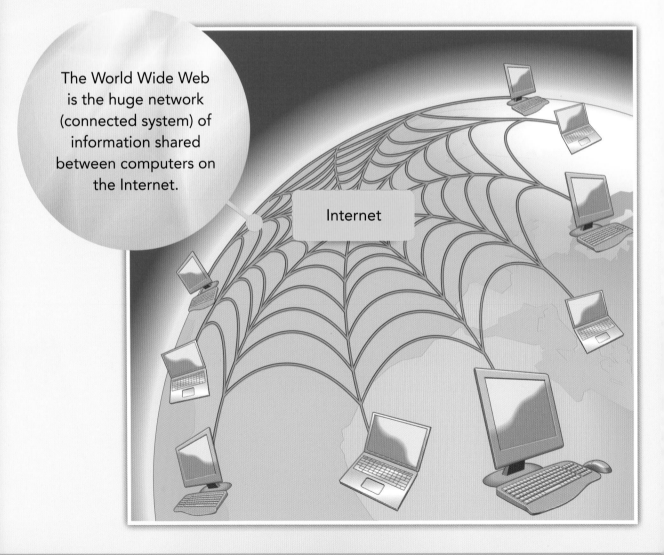

The World Wide Web is the huge network (connected system) of information shared between computers on the Internet.

Internet

Surfing the Web

When you use the Internet to search for elephants, a page will open with information all about elephants. This page is called a **Web page**. There are billions of Web pages on the Internet. They each contain different information. The **World Wide Web** is all of the Web pages of information on the Internet.

Stay safe

The Internet can be dangerous. Remember these tips:

* Never give out personal information, such as where you live, to anyone on the Internet.

* Tell an adult if anything you see on the Internet makes you feel uncomfortable.

* Never post or send pictures of yourself on the Internet without a parent or guardian's permission.

Web page   any of the pages that make up the World Wide Web
World Wide Web   all of the pages of information on the Internet

Masters of Communication

While many animals can **communicate**, humans have the most developed **language** system. Language and the alphabet are the most important **communication** technologies of all. Language allows humans to work together.

Print it

The invention of the **printing press** allowed people everywhere to be educated. Before the printing press, books were very expensive and very rare. Without many available books, most people never learned to read.

Electricity

The discovery of **electricity** allowed human beings to develop **telegraphs**, **telephones**, radios, **televisions**, and computers. Electricity allowed information to travel around the world very quickly.

No strings attached

Radio waves carry information from one place to another without wires. Radio waves can carry television sound and images from a tower on the ground to a **communications satellite** in space and back to your school in just a few seconds.

The abilities to read, write, speak, listen, see, feel, and smell are the most amazing communication technologies of all.

Try It Yourself

Build your own phone

A **telephone** can change sound into a signal. The signal travels on a wire, and it is changed back into sound by another phone. You can easily build your own phone to do this. Ask an adult for help before starting.

What you need

- 2 paper cups
- string
- a sharpened pencil

What to do

1. With the sharp pencil, poke a *small* hole through the center of the bottom of each cup.
2. Cut a piece of string as long as you like, up to about 6 ½ feet (2 meters) long.
3. Poke one end of the string through one of the paper cups and tie a knot inside the cup.
4. Repeat step 3 with the other end of the string and the other cup.

Ready, set, talk!

Do you think this phone is going to work? Will it work better with the string pulled tightly or loosely? Talk into one cup and ask a friend to see if the sound comes out through the other cup. Try it once with the string tight, and once with the string loose. Which way worked better?

voice vibrates the string

vibrations travel down the string

vibrations turn back into sound

How did it work?

Your voice vibrates (shakes) the string. These vibrations travel down the string. When they reach the other end, they vibrate the bottom of the other cup and turn back into sound.

Glossary

cell phone phone that sends wireless signals by radio waves

communicate exchange messages, thoughts, ideas, and information

communication exchange of messages, thoughts, ideas, and information

communications satellite device that flies high above Earth and sends and receives communications to and from Earth

electricity form of energy on which information and communications can be sent extremely fast, through wires

gravity natural force that pulls you back to Earth when you jump

Internet system that connects millions of computers around the world so they can share information

language set of sounds and symbols and the rules for how to use them for communication

marathon long running race named after an ancient Greek village

messenger anyone who delivers a message

Morse code code of short and long beeps used to send messages via telegraph

print markings or letters made on paper

printing press machine that allows fast printing of books and newspapers

radio wave type of energy that carries information through the air

still picture image or picture that does not move

symbol something that represents something else, such as letters

telegraph device that sends and receives electric impulses, usually in Morse code, to allow communication

telephone device that changes sound into signals and sends it to distant places, and then changes signals back into sound

television device that converts signals into moving pictures and sounds

Web page any of the pages that make up the World Wide Web

wireless signals that can be sent without the use of cords, cables, or wires—usually using radio waves

World Wide Web all of the pages of information on the Internet

Find Out More

Use these resources to find more fun and useful information about the science behind communication technologies.

Books

Graham, Ian. *Communication (Inventions in...)*. North Mankato, Minn.: QEB, 2009.

Raum, Elizabeth. *The History of the Computer (Inventions That Changed the World)*. Chicago: Heinemann Library, 2008.

Raum, Elizabeth. *The History of the Telephone (Inventions That Changed the World)*. Chicago: Heinemann Library, 2008.

Seidman, David. *Samuel Morse and the Telegraph (Inventions and Discoveries)*. North Mankato, Minn.: Capstone, 2007.

Spilsbury, Richard and Louise. *The Printing Press (Tales of Invention)*. Chicago: Heinemann Library, 2012.

Websites

http://communication.howstuffworks.com/telephone1.htm
Visit this website to learn more about how telephones work.

http://transition.fcc.gov/cgb/kidszone/history.html
This website provides fascinating histories about communication technologies such as television, the cell phone, the Internet, radio, and more.

www.classbraingames.com/2009/12/learn-morse-code
This is a great website that teaches you how to use Morse code. It also has games and activities.

www.telephonymuseum.com/telephone%20history.htm
Learn about the history of the telephone at this website.

Index